I0408775

Ultrasensitive Directional Microphone Arrays for Military Operations in Urban Terrain

Issued by Sandia National Laboratories, operated for the United States Department of Energy by Sandia Corporation.

NOTICE: This report was prepared as an account of work sponsored by an agency of the United States Government. Neither the United States Government, nor any agency thereof, nor any of their employees, nor any of their contractors, subcontractors, or their employees, make any warranty, express or implied, or assume any legal liability or responsibility for the accuracy, completeness, or usefulness of any information, apparatus, product, or process disclosed, or represent that its use would not infringe privately owned rights. Reference herein to any specific commercial product, process, or service by trade name, trademark, manufacturer, or otherwise, does not necessarily constitute or imply its endorsement, recommendation, or favoring by the United States Government, any agency thereof, or any of their contractors or subcontractors. The views and opinions expressed herein do not necessarily state or reflect those of the United States Government, any agency thereof, or any of their contractors.

Printed in the United States of America. This report has been reproduced directly from the best available copy.

Available to DOE and DOE contractors from
U.S. Department of Energy
Office of Scientific and Technical Information
P.O. Box 62
Oak Ridge, TN 37831

Telephone: (865) 576-8401
Facsimile: (865) 576-5728
E-Mail: reports@adonis.osti.gov
Online ordering: http://www.osti.gov/bridge

Available to the public from
U.S. Department of Commerce
National Technical Information Service
5285 Port Royal Rd.
Springfield, VA 22161

Telephone: (800) 553-6847
Facsimile: (703) 605-6900
E-Mail: orders@ntis.fedworld.gov
Online order: http://www.ntis.gov/help/ordermethods.asp?loc=7-4-0#online

SAND2007-7419
Unlimited Release
Printed Month Year

Ultrasensitive Directional Microphone Arrays for Military Operations in Urban Terrain

Murat Okandan, Eric P. Parker, Neal A. Hall, Ken Peterson, Paul Resnick, Darwin Serkland

Sandia National Laboratories
P.O. Box 5800
Albuquerque, New Mexico 87185

Abstract

Acoustic sensing systems are critical elements in detection of sniper events. The microphones developed in this project enable unique sensing systems that benefit significantly from the enhanced sensitivity and extremely compact foot-print. Surface and bulk micromachining technologies developed at Sandia have allowed the design, fabrication and characterization of these unique sensors. We have demonstrated sensitivity that is only available in ½ inch to 1 inch studio reference microphones - with our devices that have only 1 to 2mm diameter membranes in a volume less than $1cm^3$.

ACKNOWLEDGEMENTS

Work on this project has been carried out in collaboration with Dr. F. Levent Degertekin's group at Mechanical Engineering Department, Georgia Institute of Technology.

CONTENTS

FIGURES

1. INTRODUCTION

Interferometric displacement detection is one of the most sensitive measurement techniques, providing the basis of many scientific and commercial instruments. An extreme example is the gravitational observatories, such as Laser Interferometer Gravity-wave Observatory (LIGO, with 10^{-18} m displacement resolution). In this experiment, the interferometer arms are 4km long, enclosed in high-vacuum beam-paths, forming possibly the largest interferometer on earth.

The optical microphones described here use the same basic detection technique, as shown in Fig. 1 below, providing $40*10^{-15}$ m/√Hz displacement detection sensitivity (and $\sim 10^{-6}$ Pa/√Hz pressure sensitivity) in a volume much less than 1cm^3.

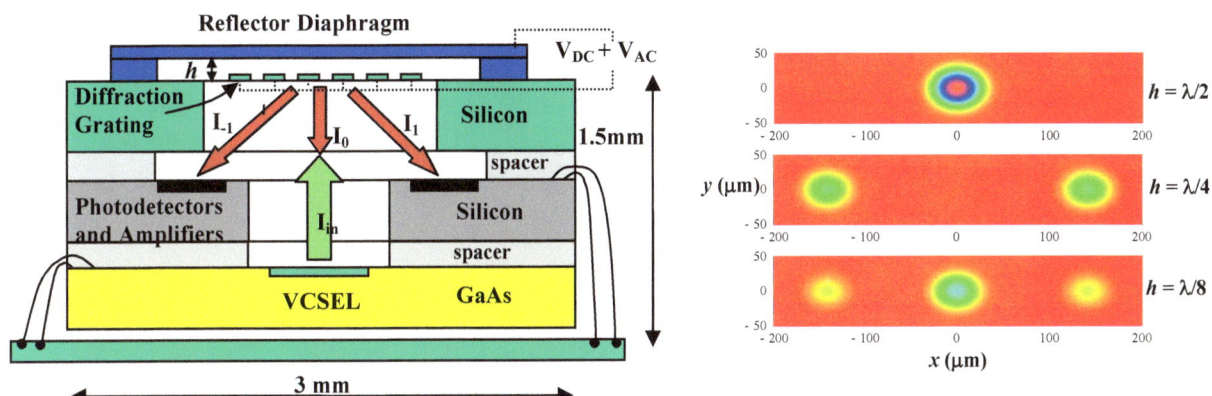

Figure 1. Schematic of an acoustic array element with integrated diffraction based optical displacement detection. Near field analysis of the diffracted field for three different gap heights *h* between the diffraction grating and the diaphragm is shown on the right side.

In this detection setup, the diffracted and reflected beams come back to fixed positions based on the wavelength used and the pitch of the diffraction grating which makes the assembly and operation of the photodetectors much simpler. The orders change their intensity based on the displacement of the diaphragm, and the 0th order (reflected beam, in the center) and the +1/-1 orders are modulated out-of-phase by this displacement.

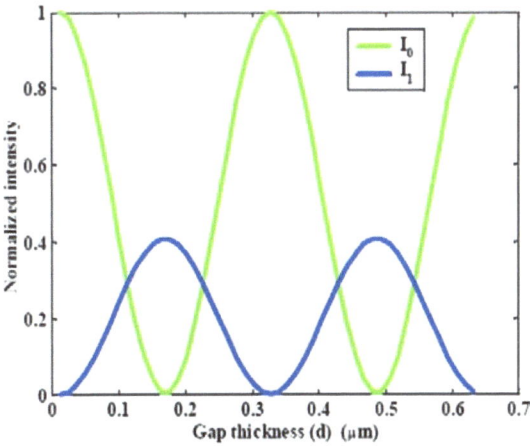

Figure 2. Variation of the order intensities with variation of gap height between reflector and grating.

The basic physical principles described above have allowed us to design, fabricate and characterize sub-cm^3 volume microphone elements that have the same sensitivity as ½'' to 1'' diameter reference microphones. Such high sensitivity microphones are used in the currently available sniper detection and tracking systems which are mostly vehicle mounted and are not soldier-portable.

Figure 3. Examples of sniper detection systems employing standard microphones in 3D array format.

Devices developed in this project are ideally suited for further improvement and miniaturization of such systems.

An additional capability that becomes viable with these sensors is the tracking of other acoustic sources and acoustic fingerprinting. A steerable acoustic sensor array enhances the possibility of detection and tracking of acoustic sources, in comparison to stand-alone omni-directional microphones.

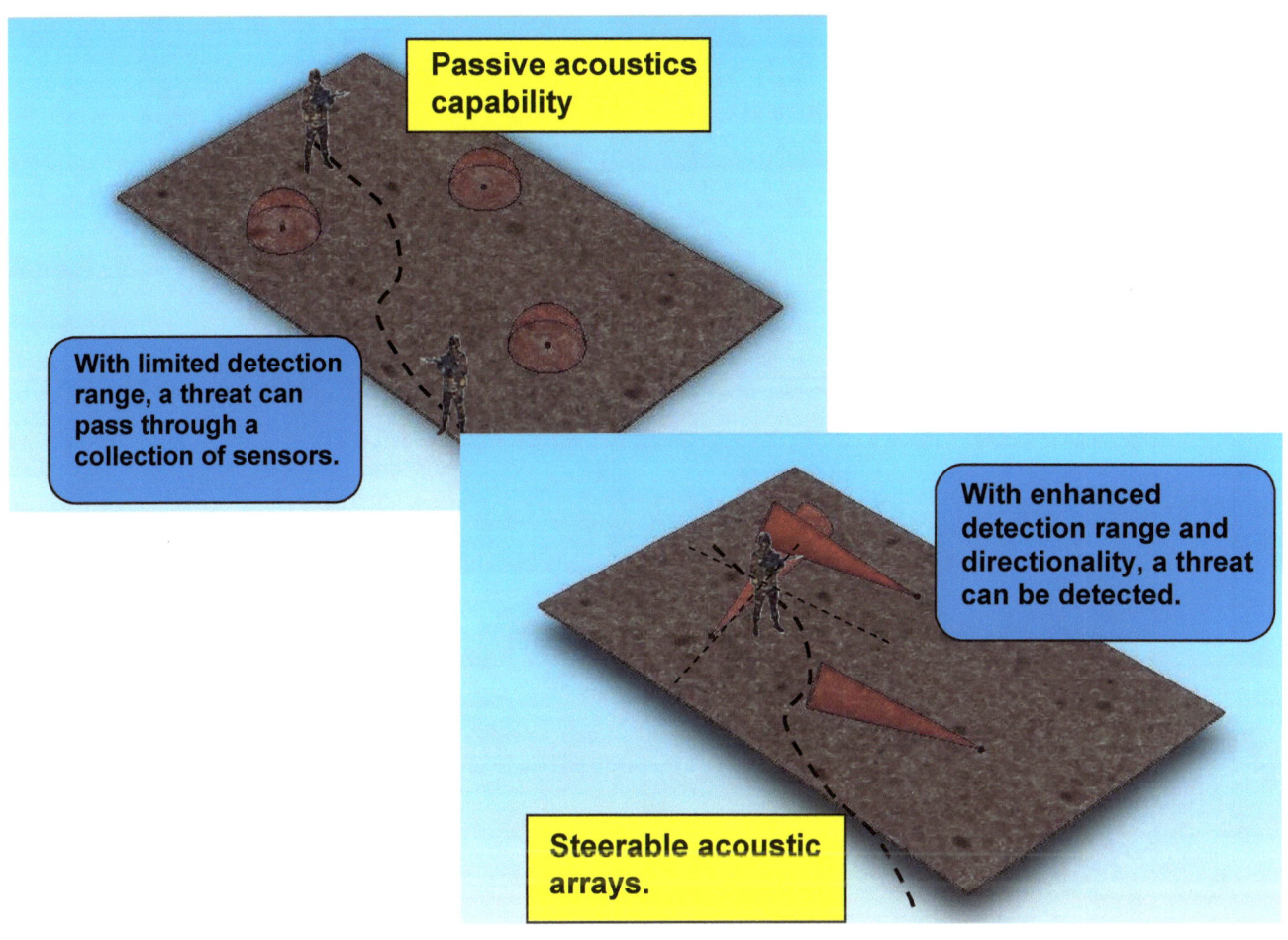

Figure 4. Possible use of the enhanced sensitivity, steerable acoustic arrays in source localization and tracking.

The sections of this report are organized as follows:

Section 2 : Device designs and fabrication

Section 3 : Packaging

Section 4 : Characterization

Section 5 : Conclusions.

2. DEVICE DESIGNS AND FABRICATION

There are 6 reticle sets (RS) with multiple design variations in each reticle, and these are described in the following sections. Some of the designs have utilized modified process flows, which are also highlighted in these sections.

2.1 RS524

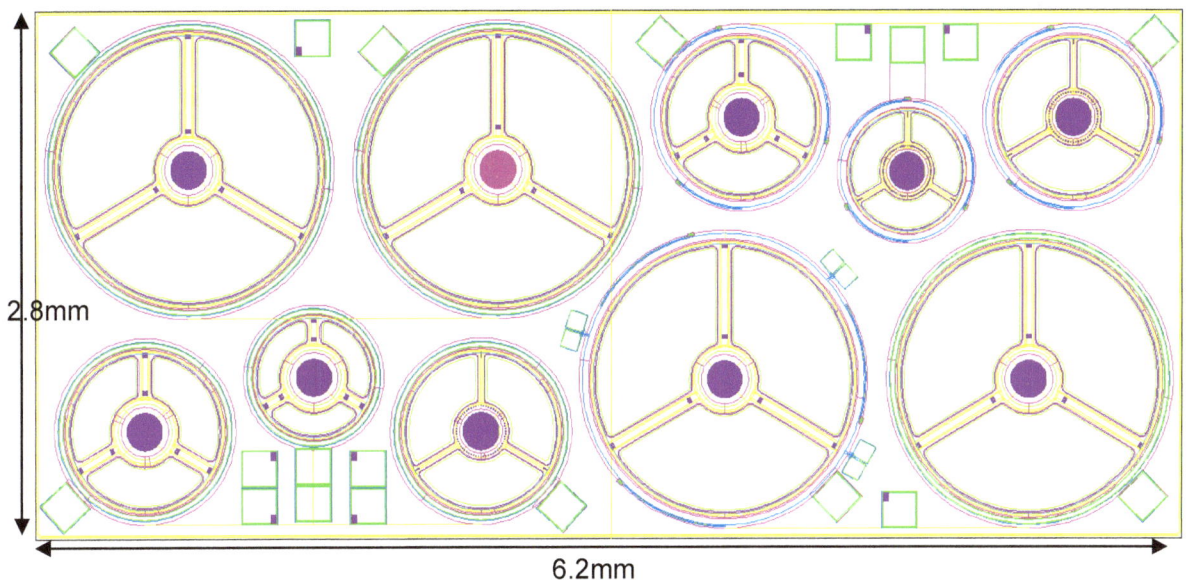

Figure 5. AutoCAD layout of microphones in RS524

These devices were fabricated using SUMMiT-lite process flow. A representative cross section is shown in Fig. 6. The top blue layer is the reflector diaphragm, which is removed in the second cross-section to highlight the grating section in the middle of the device and 3 substrate silicon support arms.

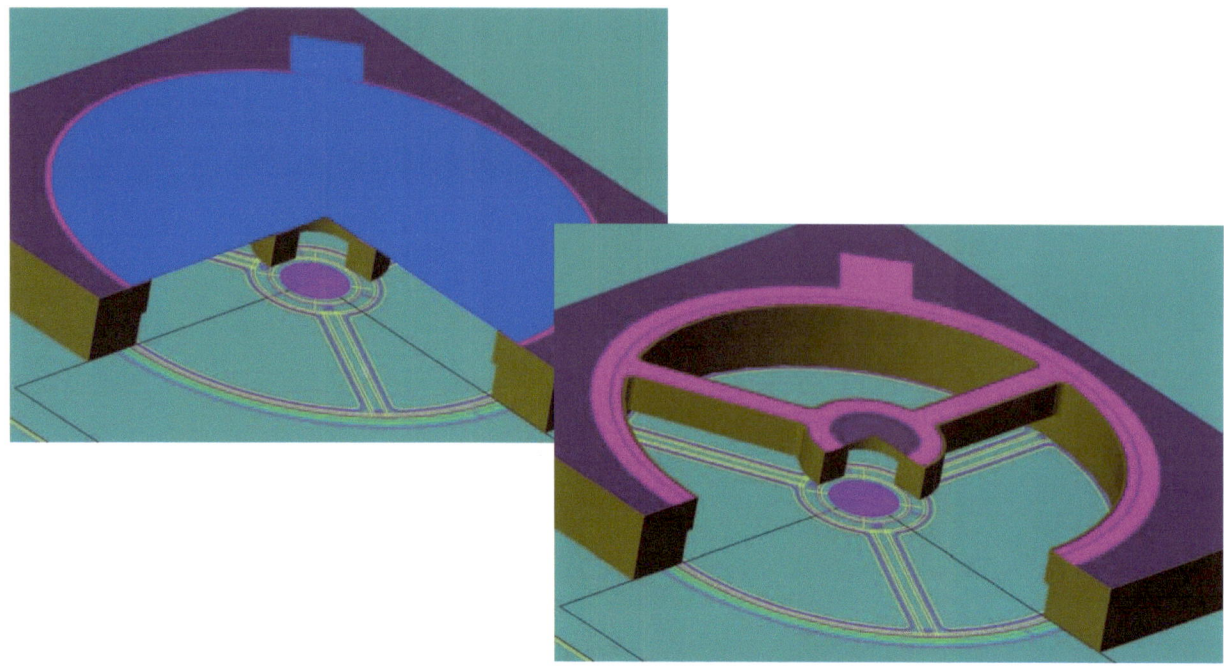

Figure 6. 3D cross-section of 1.5mm diameter membrane microphone.

In the fabrication process splits, there were 3 different oxide thicknesses (which determined the initial gap height between the diaphragm and the grating) – A:3um, B:4.5um, C:6um.

After release etch (which removes the sacrificial oxide), these devices were gold coated (10nm tungsten, 100nm gold) from the back side to improve the reflectivity of the grating and the diaphragm.

2.2 RS569

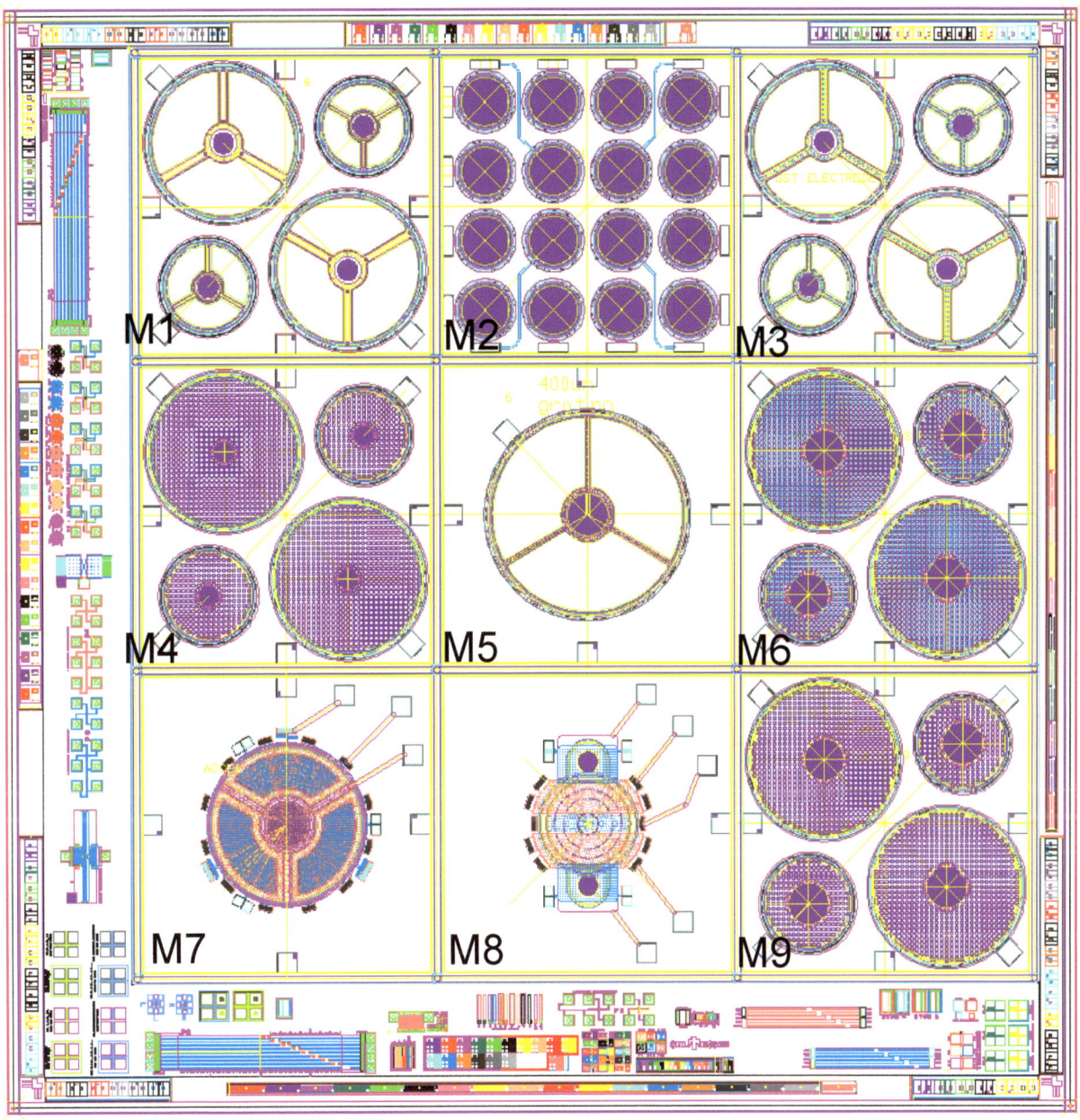

Figure 7. RS569 full reticle set.

Except for modules 7 and 8, all of the devices were microphone design variations. The process flow was SUMMiT-lite, with 0.3um poly0, 6um total sacrificial oxide, 2.25um poly3 and 2.25um thick poly4 (top layer). Each module is 3mm x 3mm in size and gratings are composed of 2um silicon nitride fingers (0.8um thick) and 2um spaces.

M1

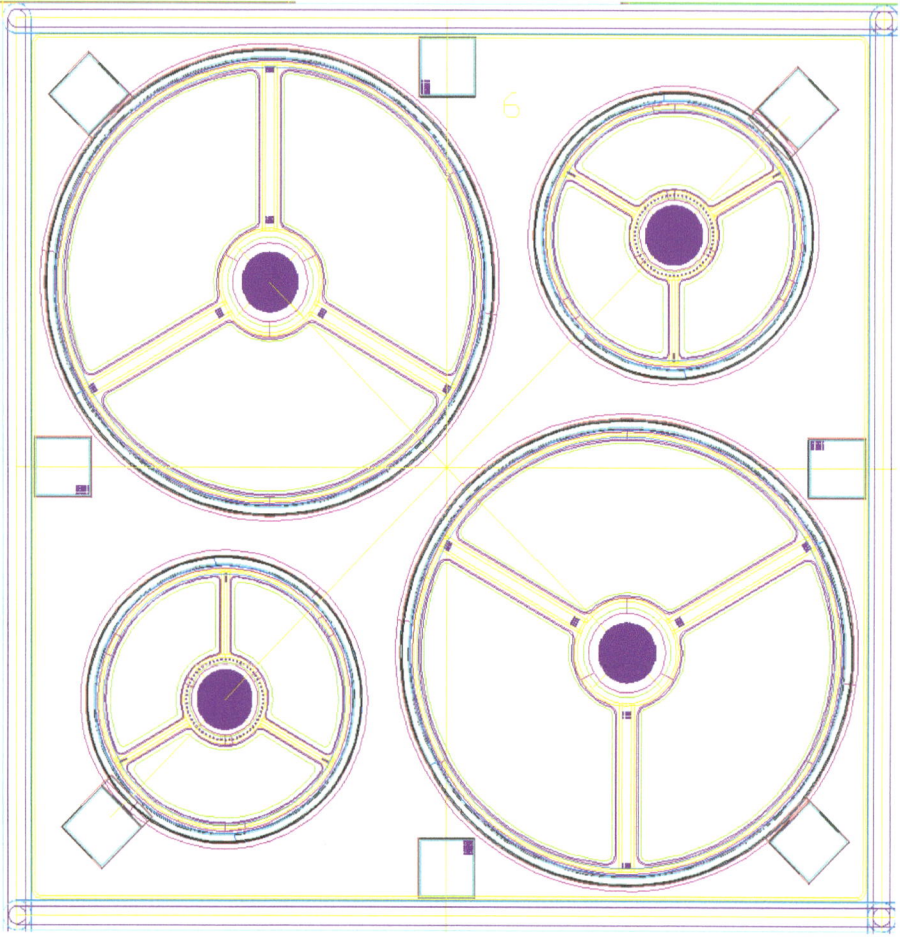

Figure 8. RS569 – module1

These are 1.5mm and 0.9mm diameter microphones, with 200um diameter grating structures. Support arms for the 1.5mm device are 100um wide, and 70um wide for the 0.9mm device.

M2

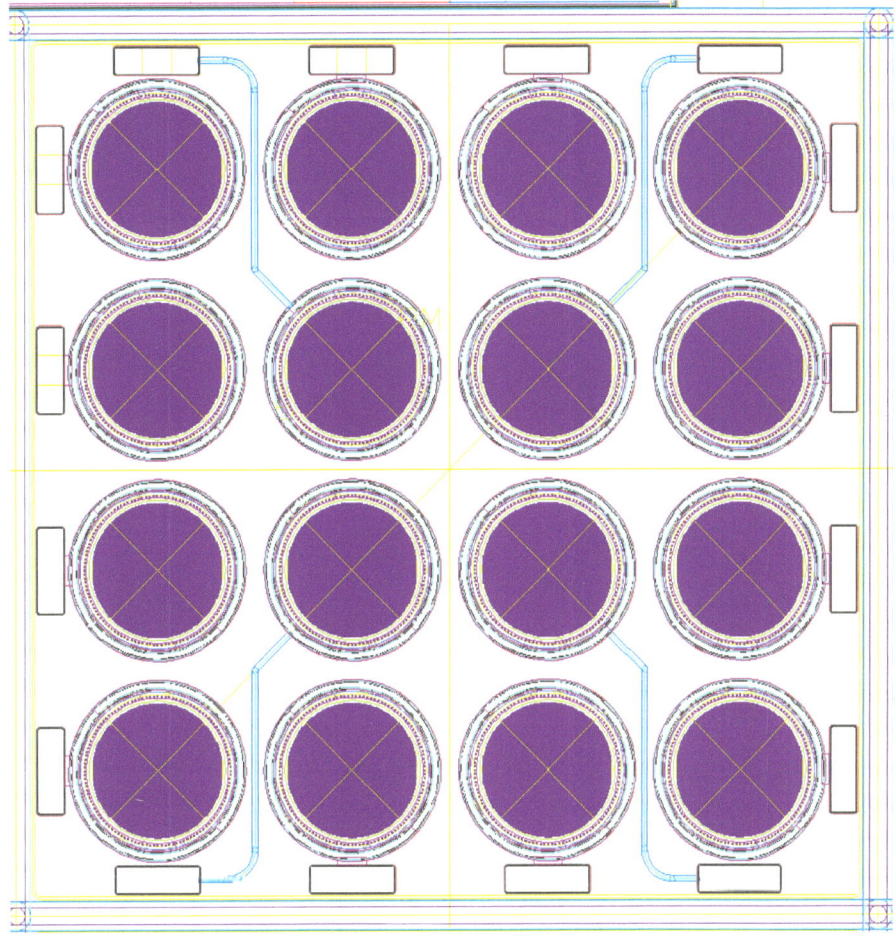

Figure 9. RS569 – module 2

Module 2 is a 4x4 array of 550um diameter microphones. There are no support arms below the diaphragm, all of the space is taken up by the grating. Top electrode (diaphragm) connections are pulled to the edge of the die for easier wire-bond access. Device substrate is common for all devices.

M3

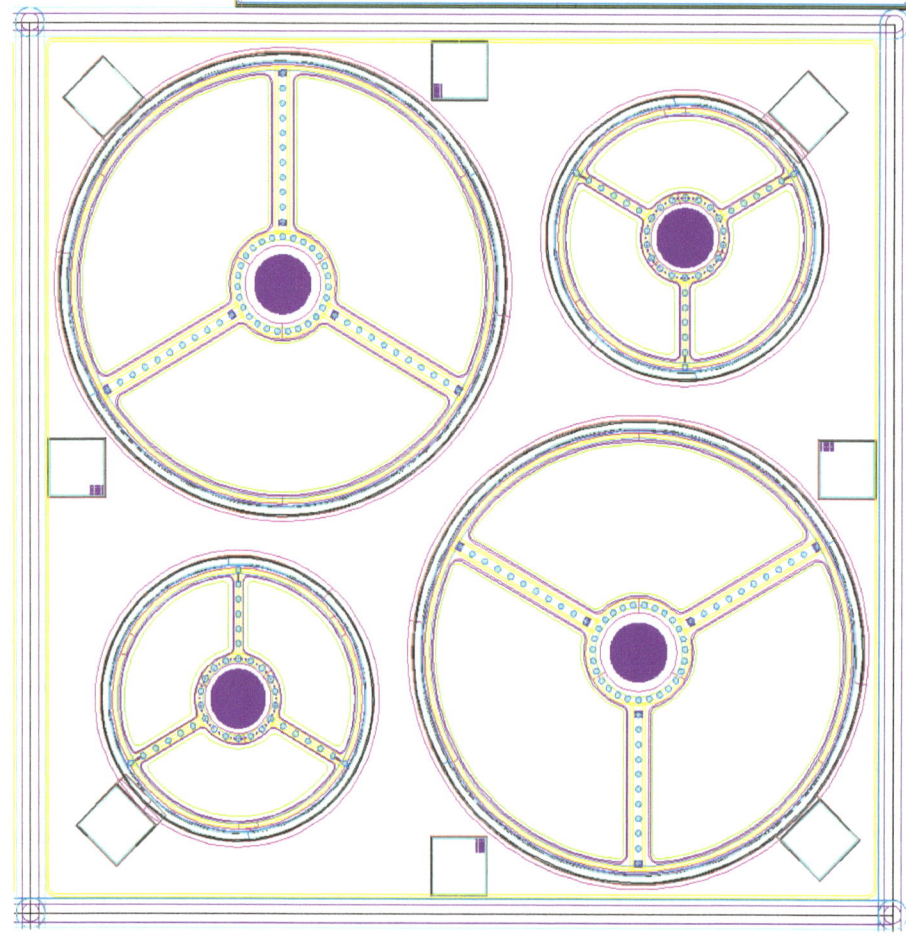

Figure 10. RS569 – module 3

Module 3 has the same devices (1.5mm and 0.9mm diameter) as in module1, with the added post style electrodes on the grating support arms that go up to poly3 layer (2.25um thick poly, top of poly 2um below the diaphragm). This will allow the membrane to be actuated at lower voltages compared to the devices in module1.

M4

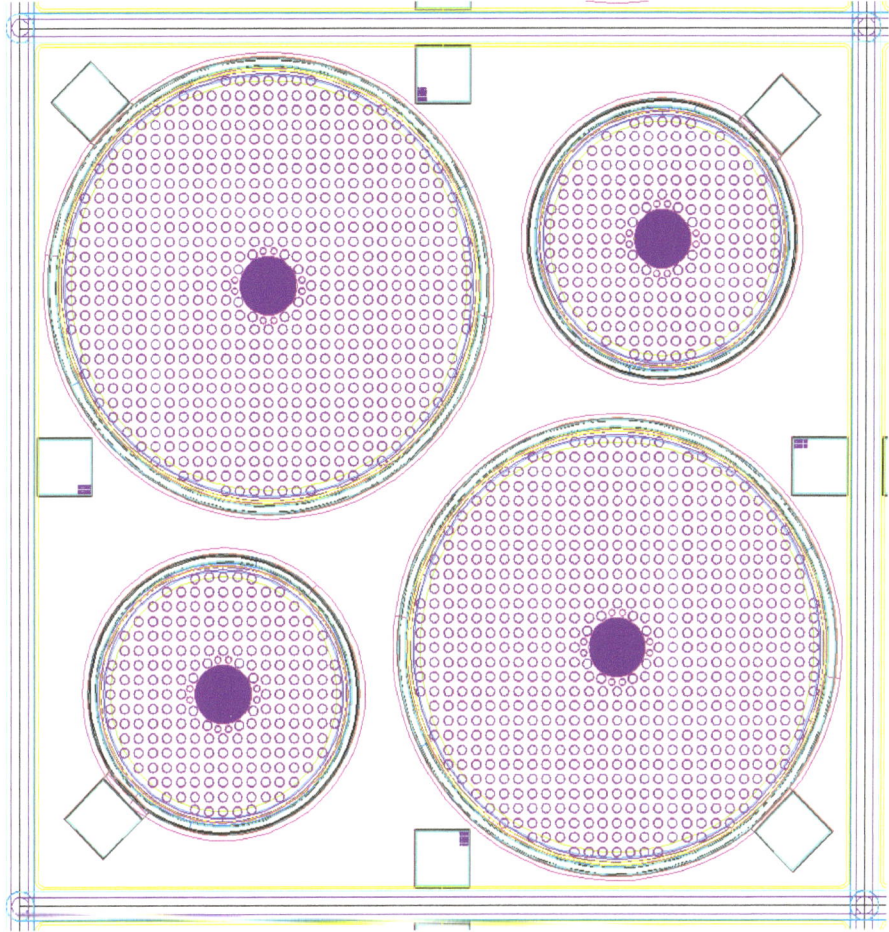

Figure 11. RS569 – module 4

Devices in module 4 have the same diaphragm size as the devices in module 1, but the grating support structure is modified to be nitride only. The circular cut-outs are similar to the more traditional microphone back-plate designs, and the grating size is 200um. The bottom electrode (poly0) is present throughout the nitride except over the nitride-cut regions and the grating region.

M5

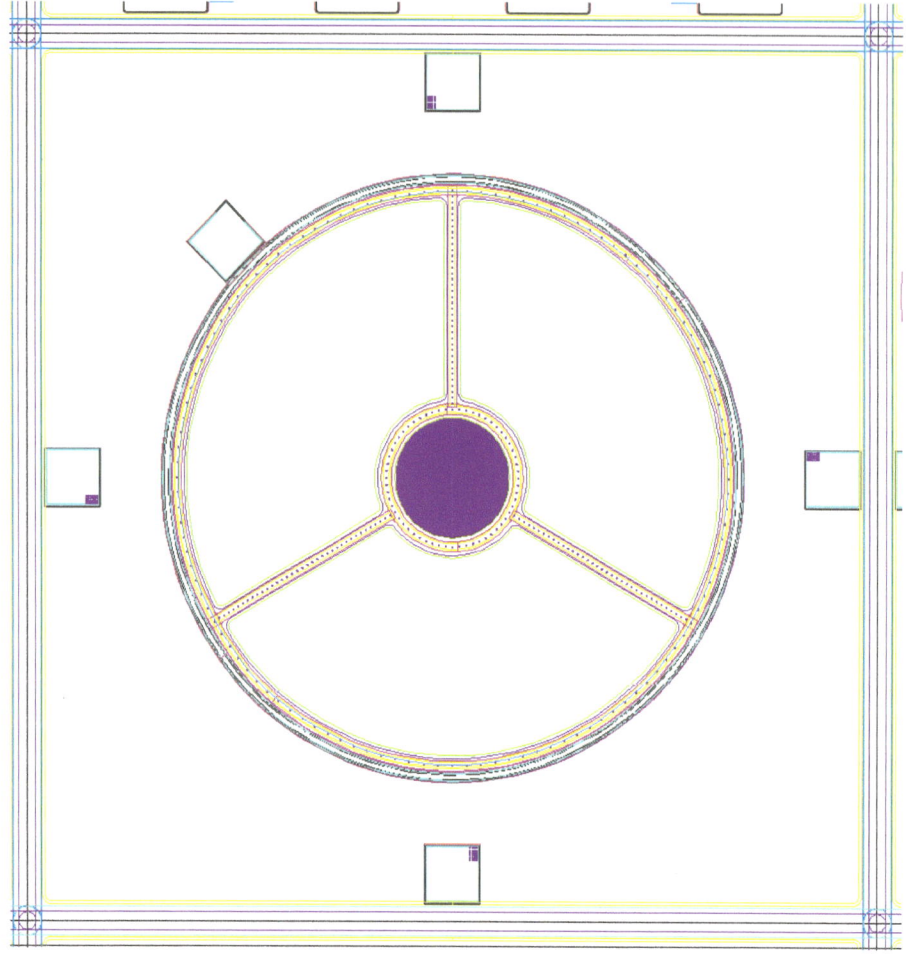

Figure 12. RS569 – module 5

This device has a 2mm diameter diaphragm. Also, the grating is 400um in diameter and the support arms are 60um wide.

M6

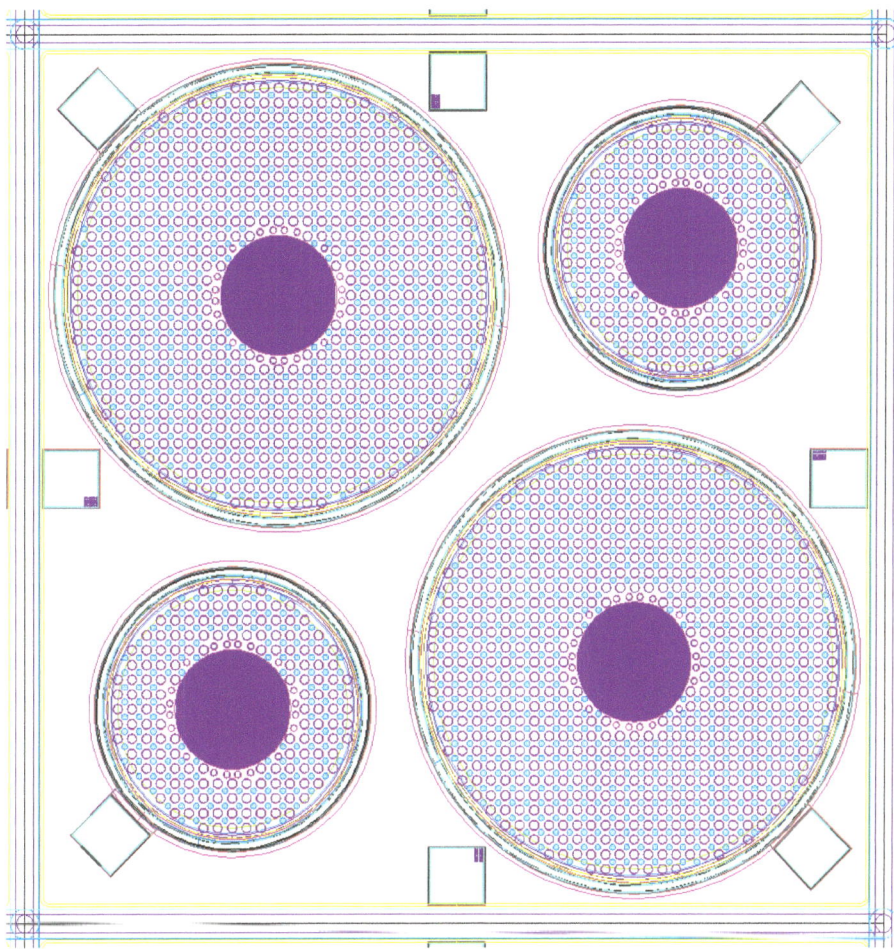

Figure 13. RS569 – module 6

These devices are identical to the nitride backplate designs as in module 4, the modifications are larger gratings (400um diameter) and poly3 post electrodes, tied to poly0 and substrate for all devices.

M9

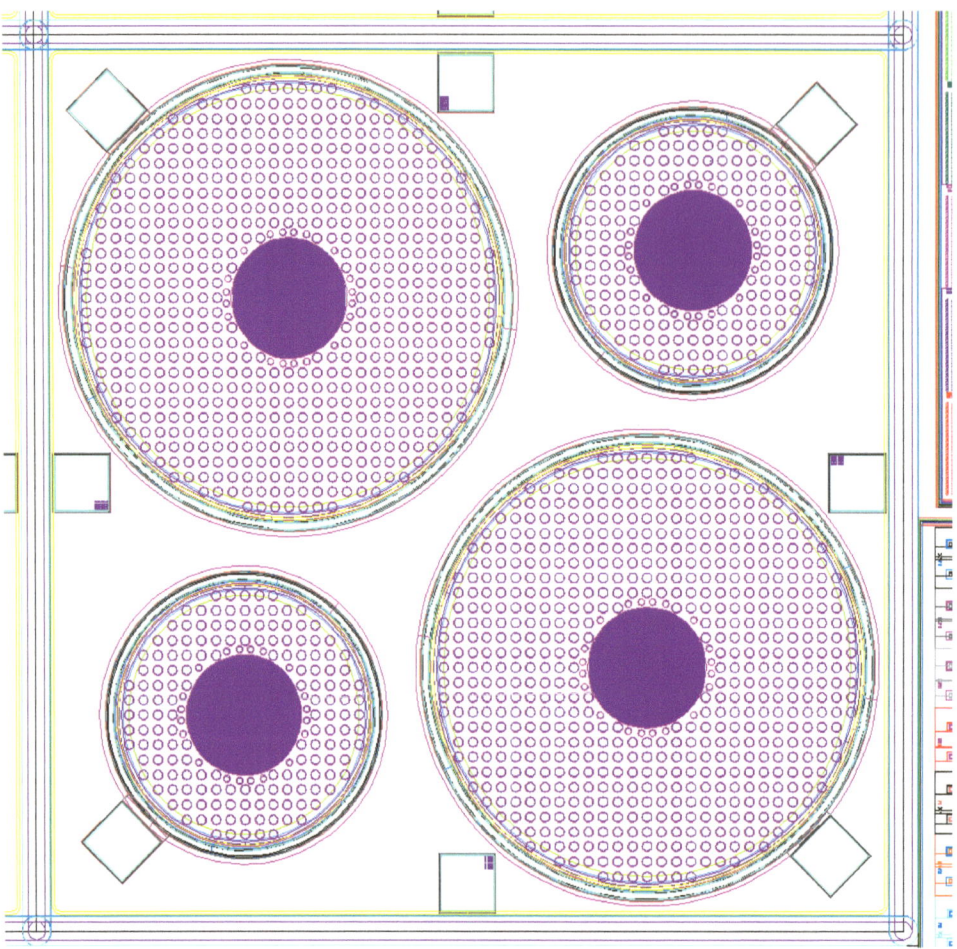

Figure 14. RS569 – module 9

Devices in module9 are the same design as in module 6 except the poly3 post electrodes and the gratings are 400um in diameter.

2.3 RS575

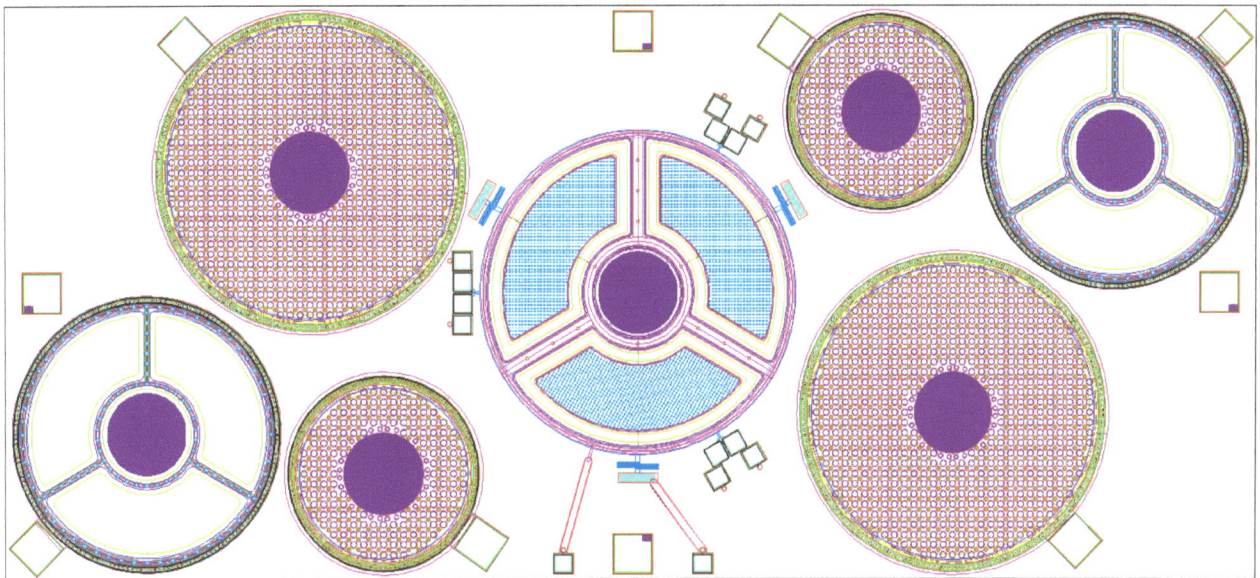

Figure 15. RS575 – microphone module

Devices at the corners of this module are the microphones and there is an accelerometer design in the center of the module. All gratings are nitride (0.8um thick) and 2um line and space. This module was fabricated in a standard SUMMiTV process flow.

There are two nitride backplate designs (1.5mm and 0.9mm diameter diaphragms), with poly3 post electrodes. The support arms for the silicon backplate designs are 80um wide, with 1.2mm diameter diaphragms. There are also poly3 post electrodes on these support arm structures.

Another feature in this design is the static pressure vents that are lithographically defined (3um diameter) and are etched onto the diaphragms. This allows a much more uniform low frequency cut-off performance across these designs. The vents are replicated at 3 positions around the periphery of each device.

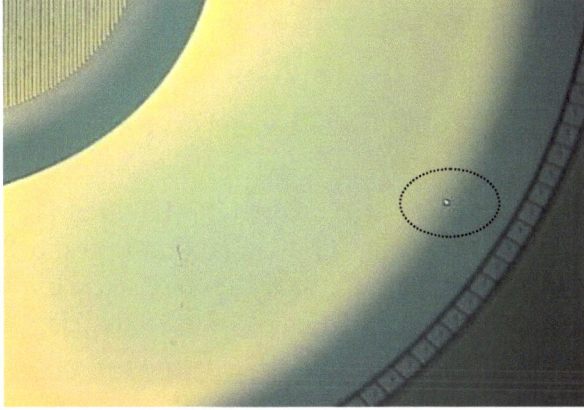

Figure 16. Static pressure equalization port (3um diameter) on microphone diaphragm.

2.4 RS620

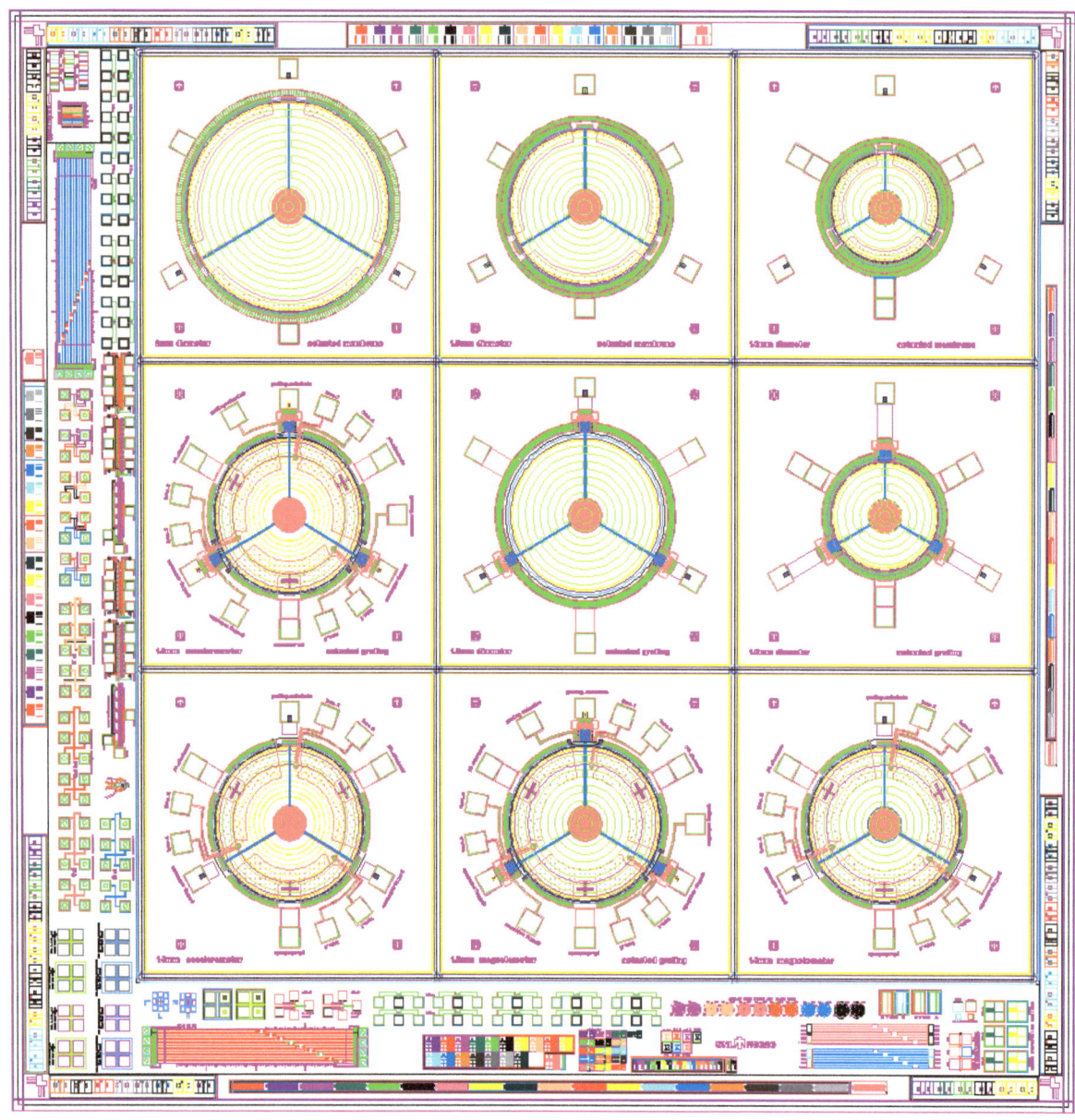

Figure 17. RS620 full reticle set

This reticle set used a process flow similar to RS524, SUMMiT-lite. Modules 1-3, 5 and 6 are different microphone designs. One important variation is that the grating structure is made in the top layer (poly4) rather than in nitride. This allows a 1um line/space grating to be formed with 400um diameter. The diaphragm is polysilicon, 0.6 or 1.3um thick, depending on the process split.

M1

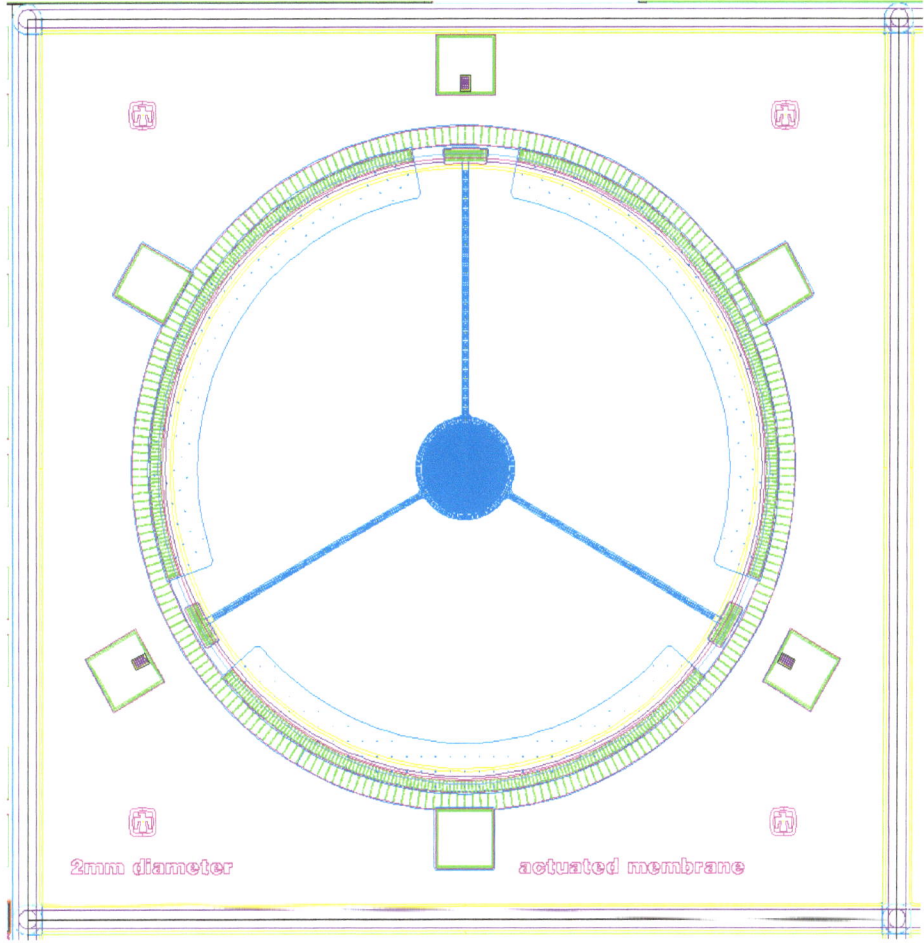

Figure 18. RS620 – module 1

This is a 2.0 mm diameter diaphragm microphone. 400um diameter grating is on the topmost poly layer (poly3), which also has the actuation electrodes. The membrane is formed on the lowest polysilicon layers. A Bosch etch from the back side opens up the microphone to acoustic input.

M2

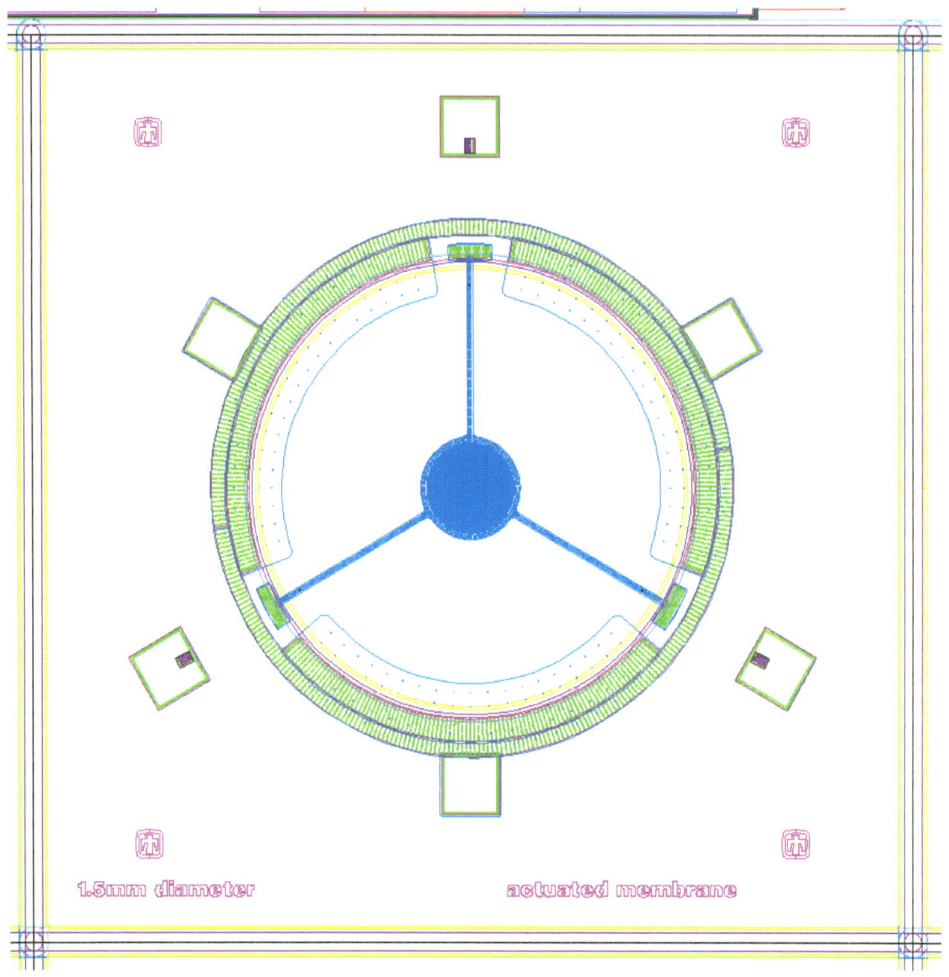

Figure 19. RS620 – module 2

This is the same design as module 1, with a 1.5 mm diameter diaphragm.

M3

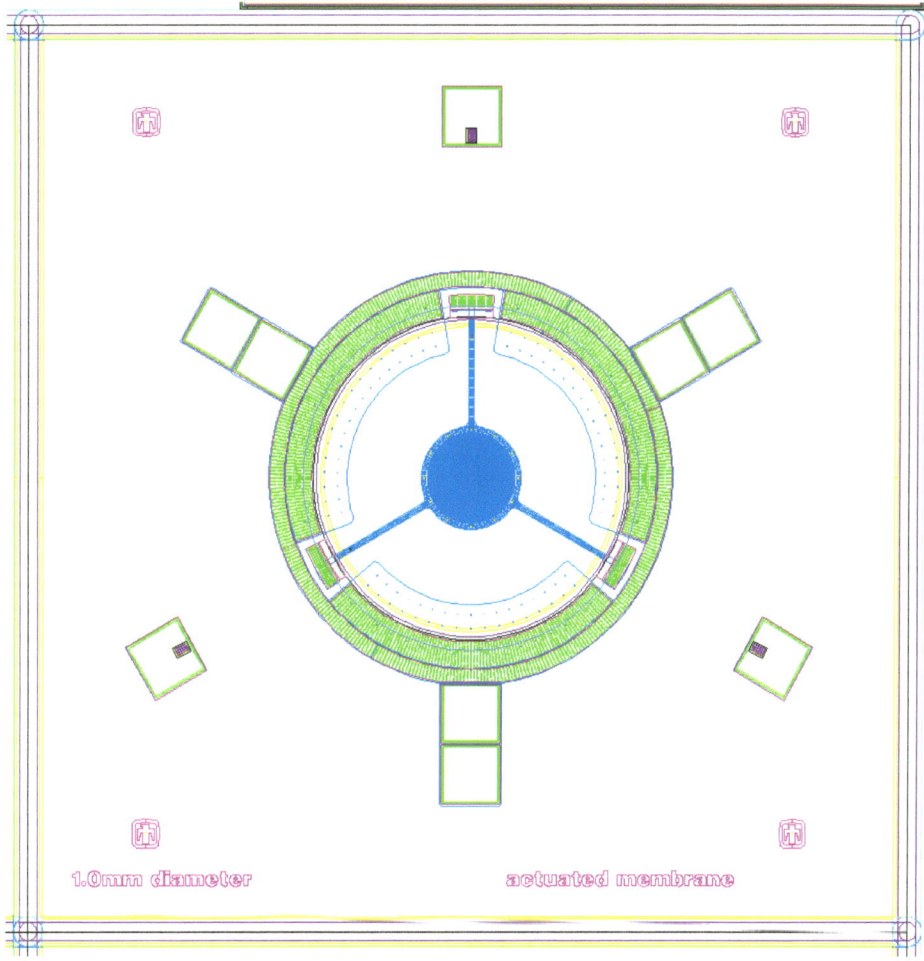

Figure 20. RS620 – module 3

This is the same design as module 1, with a 1.0 mm diameter diaphragm.

M5

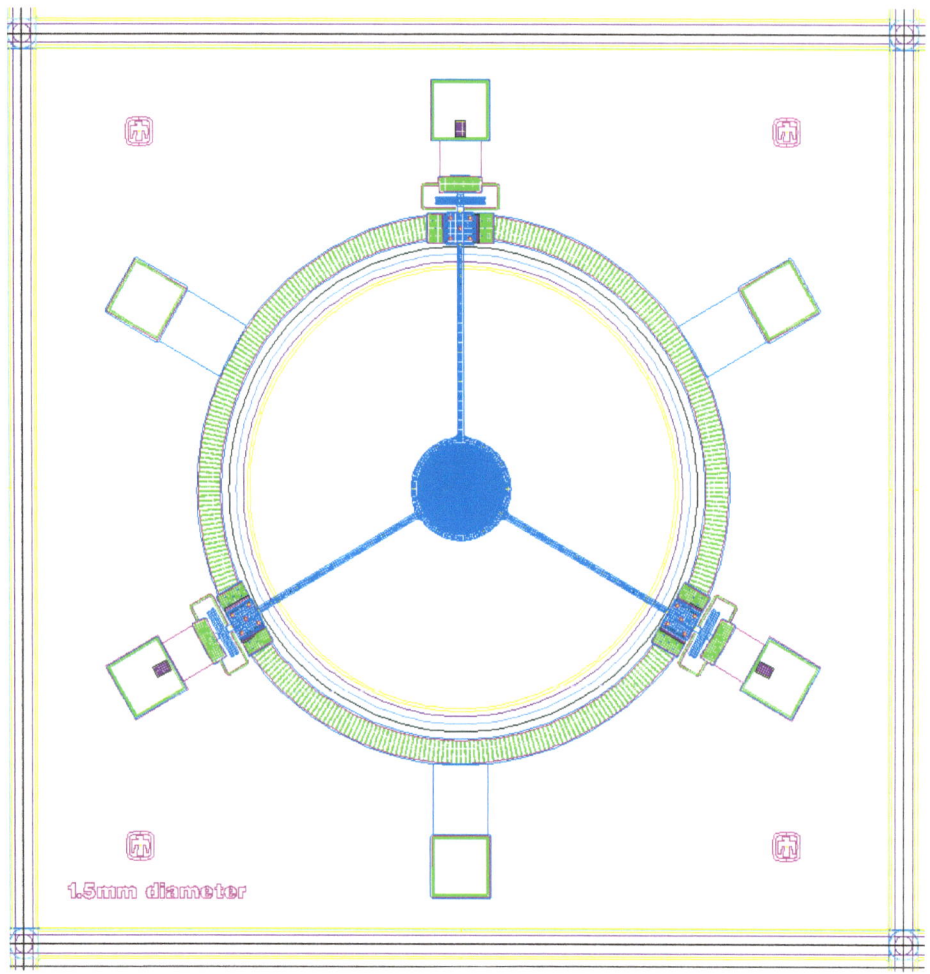

Figure 21. RS620 – module 5

This design has the same basic features as module 2, except the grating structure is suspended with a modified anchor.

M6

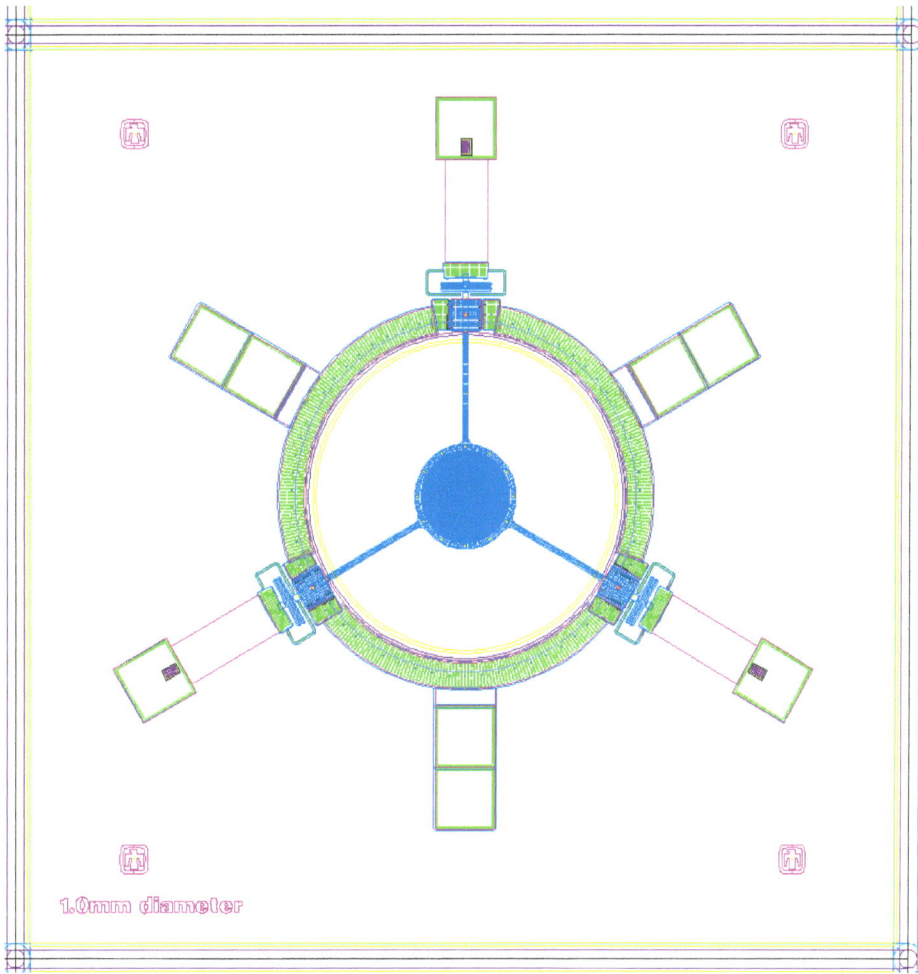

Figure 22. RS620 – module 6

This design has the same basic features as module 3, except the grating structure is suspended with a modified anchor.

2.5 RS630

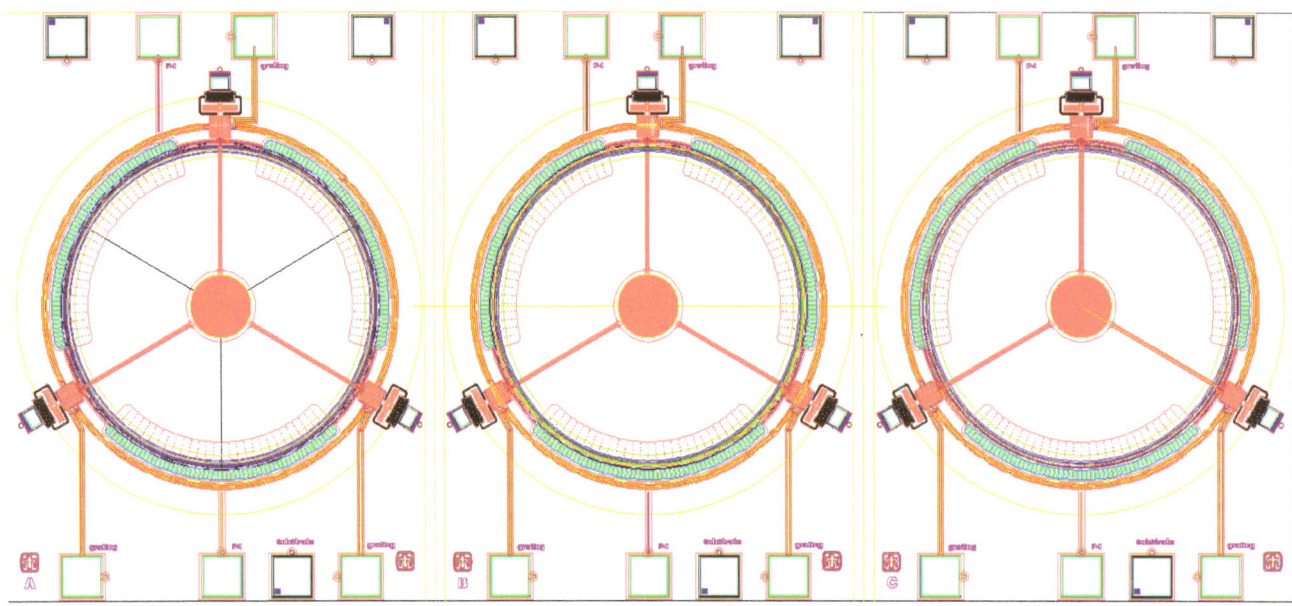

Figure 23. RS630 microphone module

This design was fabricated in SUMMiTV process flow. The grating is 400um in diameter, 1um line/space and the 1.5 mm diaphragm is formed in poly1, poly2 or poly1/poly2 laminate. The grating is suspended using a modified anchor. The static pressure vent ports are also present in these designs. With the different designs (A, B, C), various diaphragm anchoring and thickness variations are tested. A Bosch etched cavity from the back allows acoustic input into these devices.

2.6 RS646

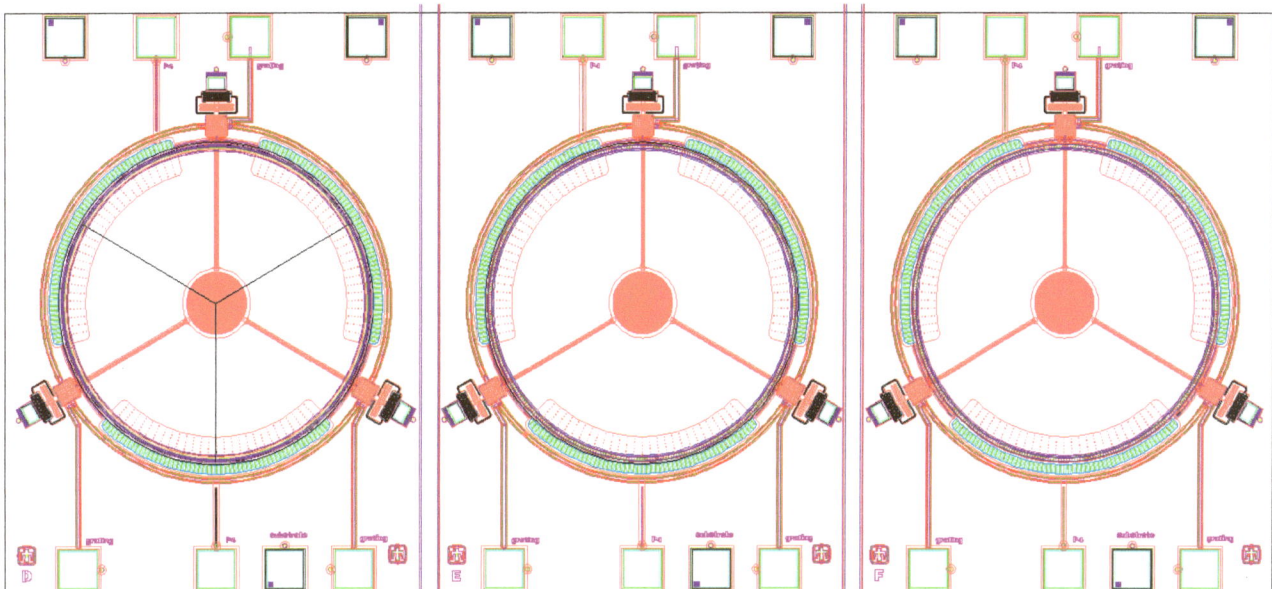

Figure 24. RS646 microphone module

This design was fabricated in SUMMiTV process flow. The features are very similar to the designs in RS630, modifications were done in the diaphragm anchoring and suspension of the grating structure. The 1.5 mm diaphragm is defined in poly2, and variations in suspensions are carried out through devices D, E and F. Gratings are 1um line/space, 400um diameter and they are defined in poly4. A Bosch etched cavity form the back side allows acoustic input into these devices.

3. PACKAGING

Some of the initial devices were characterized in a table-top optical system to determine the basic mechanical characteristics of the microphones. Standard 24-pin ceramic DIP packages were laser-cut to allow optical access from the back side of the package. Wire bonds were attached to the front side of the die and to the landing pads for the package pins.

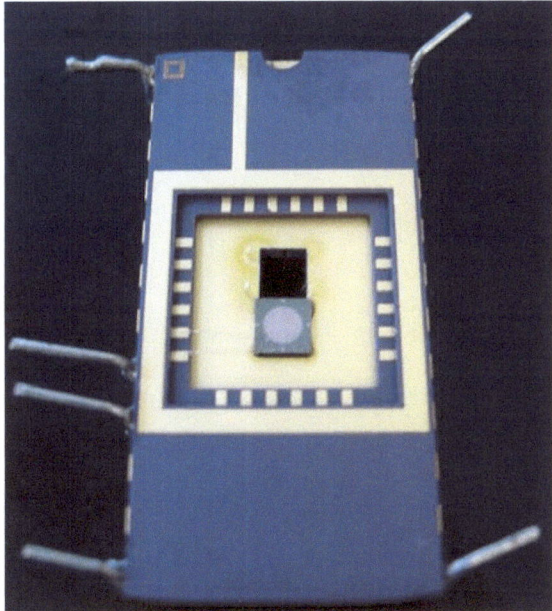 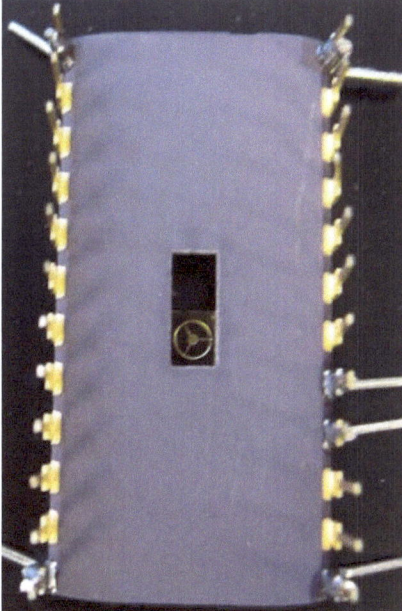

Figure 25. Microphone in modified ceramic DIP for mechanical characterization

Other parts were assembled with low temperature co-fired ceramic (LTCC) spacers and holders to accommodate the light source (VCSEL) and photodiodes in the same package.

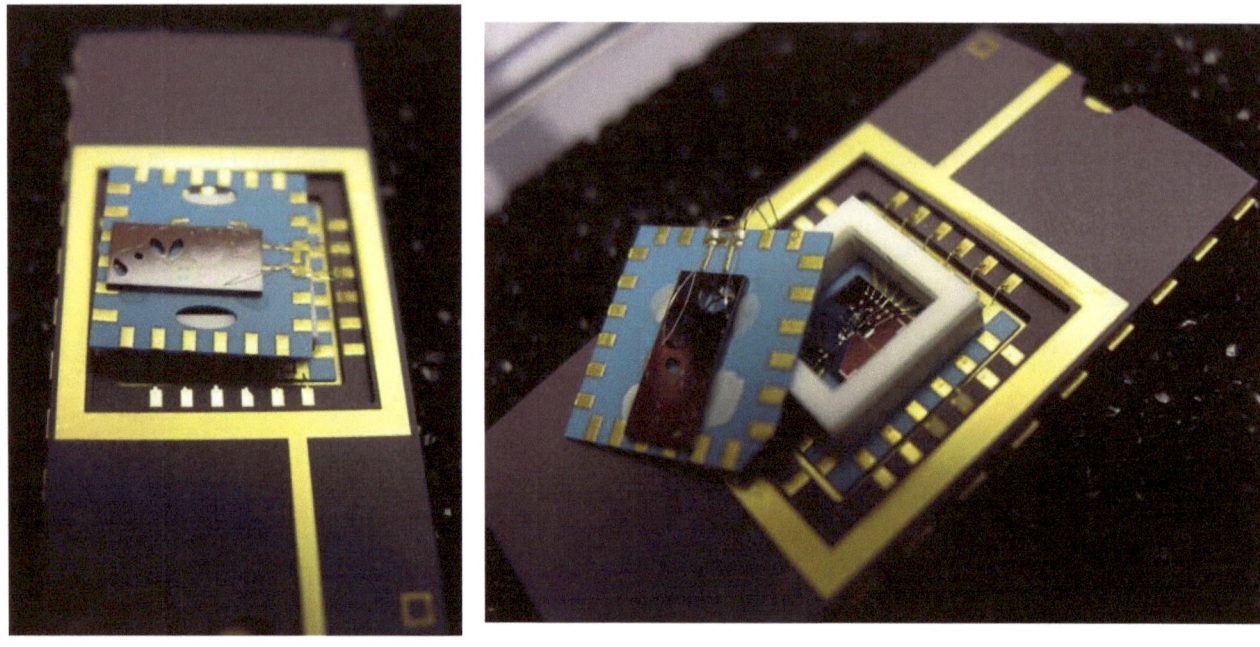

Figure 26. LTCC holders and spacers for the complete assembly

This assembly allowed characterization of parts in better controlled acoustic and mechanical environments compared to the table-top characterization setup. Same components were also leveraged for the high sensitivity accelerometer integration LDRD tests.

These assemblies made use of optical modeling programs to work out the beam paths and placement of photodiodes, microphone and the VCSEL.

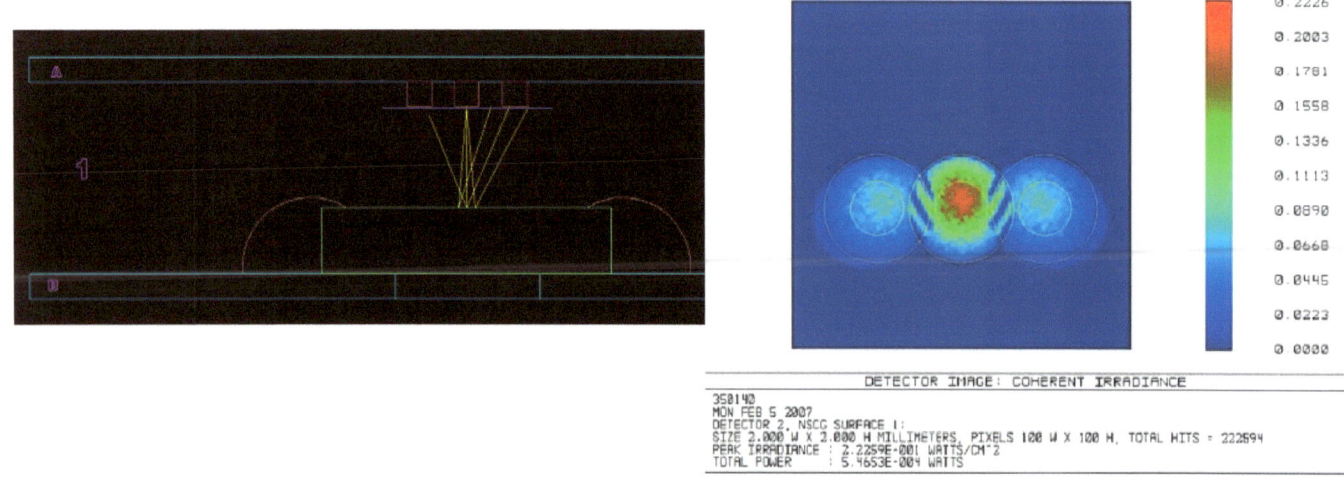

Figure 27. Sketch of component layout and modeled beam patterns on the detector.

For assembly of devices from RS620, RS630 and RS646, a silicon VCSEL and photodiode holder was also fabricated (RS621). This piece allowed the VCSEL to be assembled at a 10º angle, making the diffracted and reflected beams easier to position on the photodiodes.

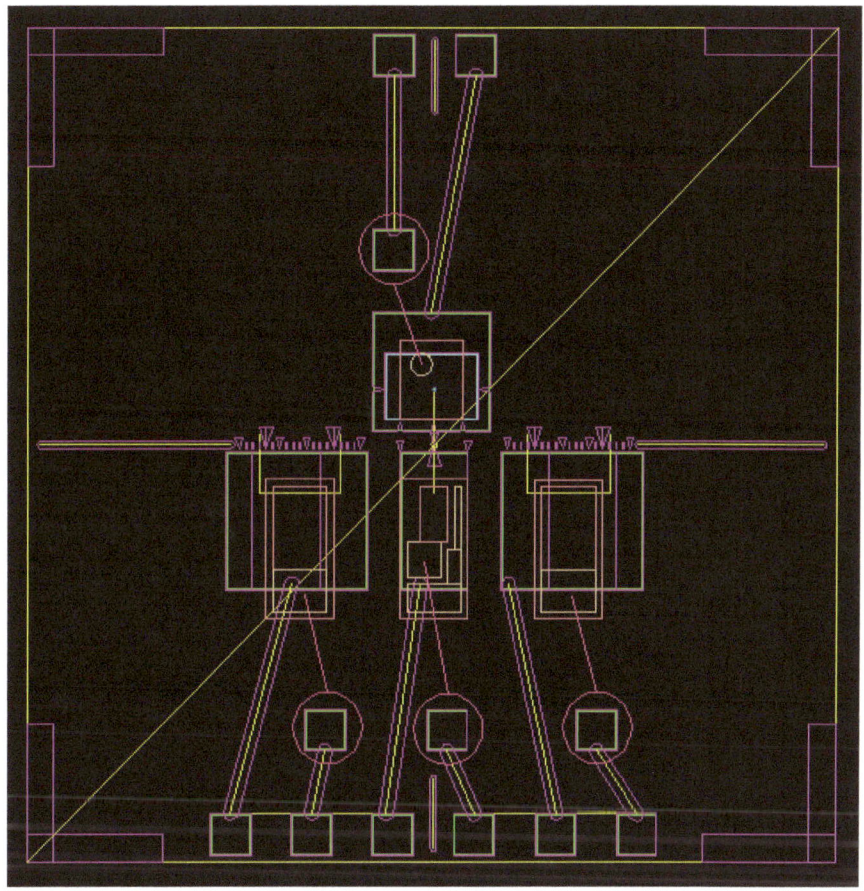

Figure 28. Silicon VCSEL and PD holder piece (RS621).

4. CHARACTERIZATION

Devices were characterized initially on a table-top system to obtain the mechanical response of the membranes (resonant frequency, compliance, etc.). After this initial phase of characterization, some of the devices were packaged further and characterized acoustically (i.e., in an anechoic chamber, at Georgia Tech). The initial characterization used stand-alone lasers, photodiodes and amplifiers. For acoustic testing and some of the demonstration devices, fully integrated assemblies (VCSEL, PDs and amplifiers inside the same package) were utilized.

4.1 Mechanical Characterization

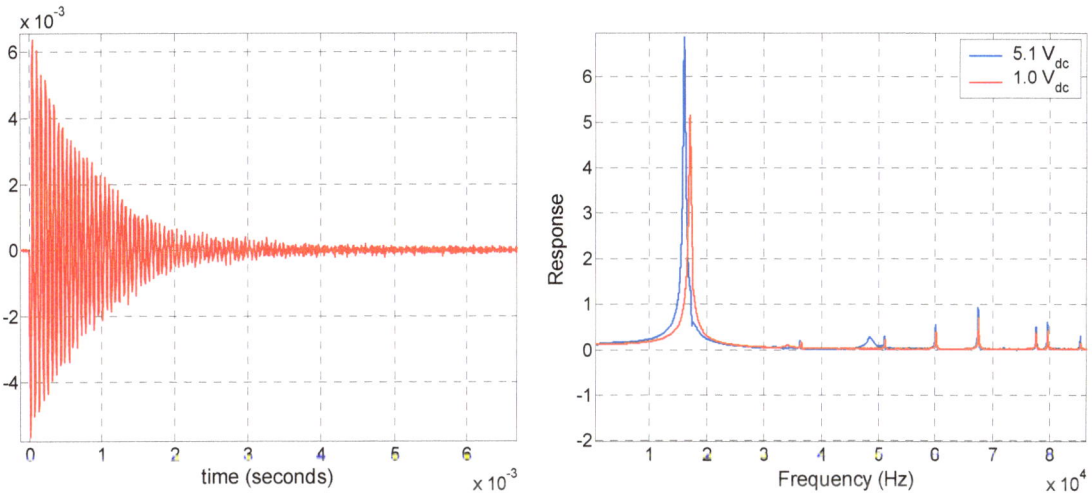

Figure 29. Impulse response (electrostatic actuation) of a 1.5mm diaphragm device from RS524 (1.25 Torr chamber pressure).

The impulse response of a 1.5mm diameter microphone from RS524 is shown in Figure 29. This test was carried out in reduced pressure (1.25 Torr) chamber in order to determine the innate mechanical properties of the microphones without the damping caused by ambient atmosphere. The dynamic response versus time and the FFT plots shown in the second graph point to a 17.5kHz resonance for the diaphragm.

Squeeze film damping is one of the critical physical effects that determine the bandwidth of these microphones. The plots in Fig. 30 show the same device with varying distances (2um, 4.5um and 6um) between the 1.5mm microphone diaphragm and the grating and support arms. For smaller gaps, squeeze film damping is higher and the bandwidth is reduced. Two traces that overlay each other correspond to two 1.5mm devices on the same chip, which illustrates one of the key benefits of micromachined microphones, devices that are made in the same process flow (same wafer, same chip) will have extremely well matched characteristics. This is a crucial requirement for devices that are used in phased array/directional applications.

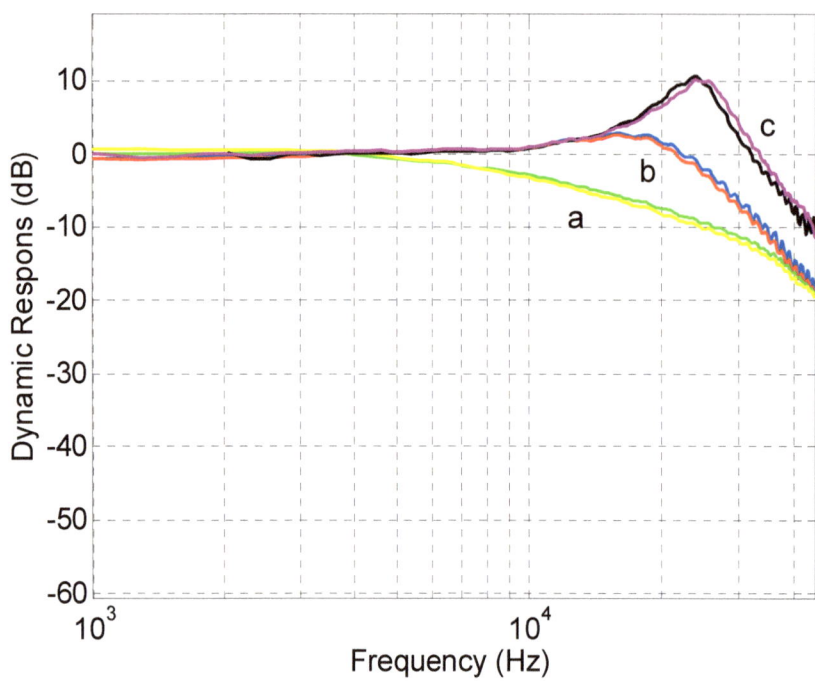

Figure 30. Dynamic response of 1.5mm devices with varying gap heights between the diaphragm and the grating/support arms (backplate), a) 2um, b) 4.5um and c) 6um.

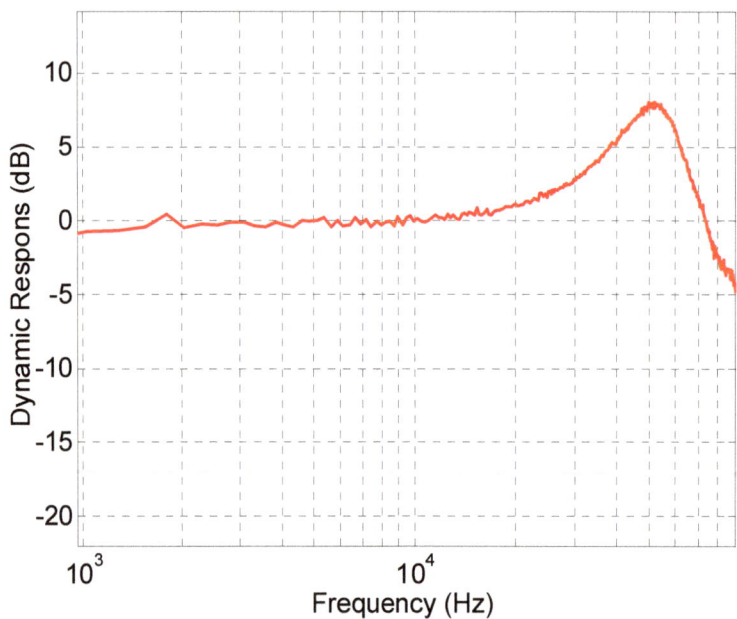

Figure 31. Dynamic response of 900um diameter diaphragm microphones.

Diaphragm size and stiffness also determines the frequency range of these microphones. For example, a 900um diameter microphone from RS524 is shown in Fig. 31. The observed resonant frequency for these devices is 50 kHz, which is ideal for high frequency source identification applications.

4.2 Acoustic Characterization

1.5mm diameter and 2mm diameter devices were packaged and tested in an anechoic chamber at Georgia Tech for determining the acoustic properties of these microphones. Figure 32 shows the prototype testing setup which houses the optoelectronics and amplifiers below the microphone.

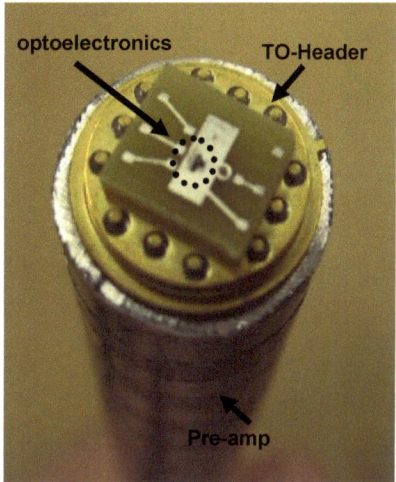

Figure 32. Prototype microphone test setup with integrated optoelectronic components.

A representative acoustic response plot is shown in Figure 33. Low frequency response is shown in more detail in Fig. 34. Acoustic response of a 2mm diameter membrane device is shown in Fig.35 with a resonant frequency around 13 kHz. The corresponding thermal pressure noise limit is 1.2uPa/√Hz (17dBA self noise) throughout the flat region of the response, which is unprecedented for a device of this size.

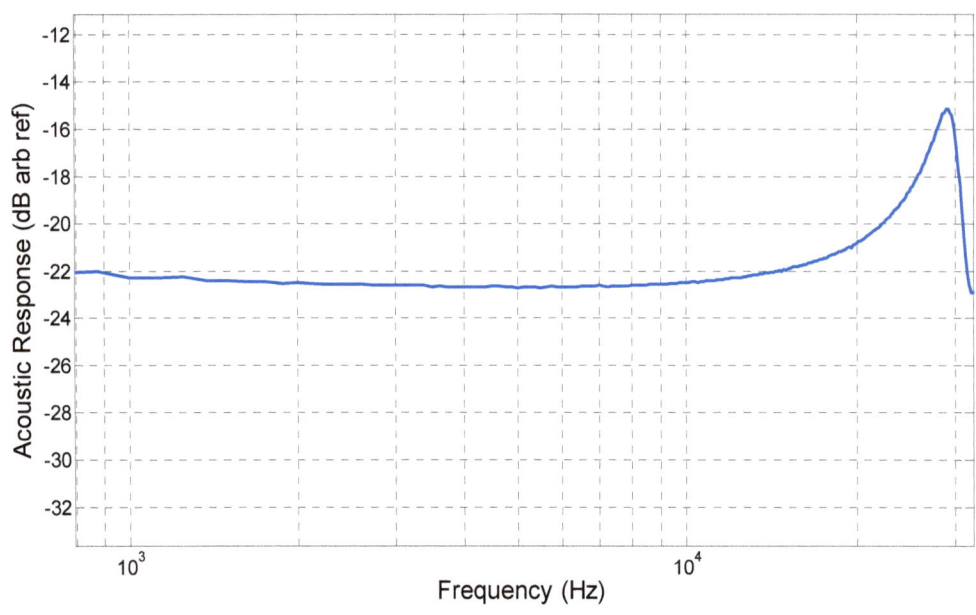

Figure 33. Acoustic response of a 1.5mm device mounted in the prototype test setup.

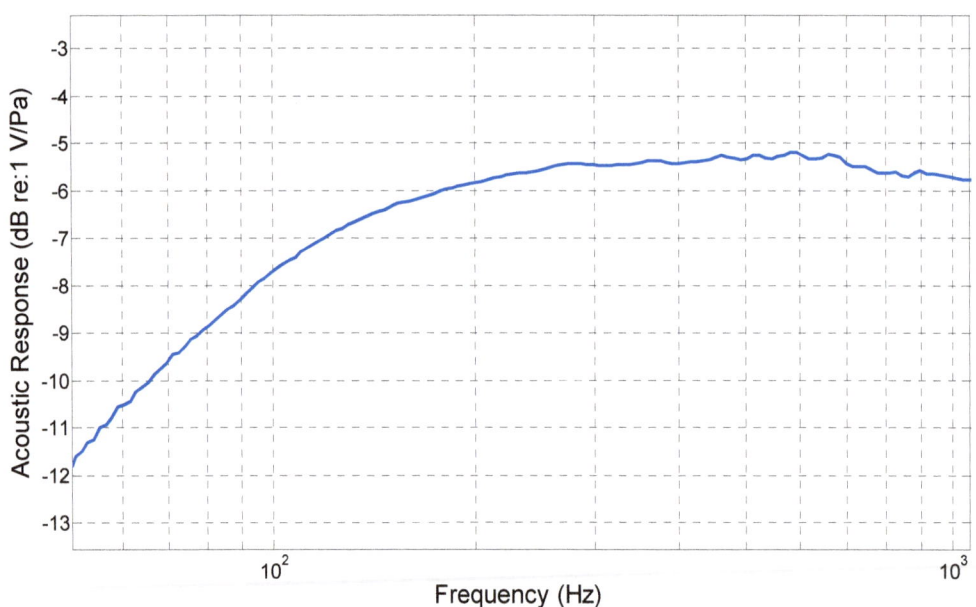

Figure 34. Low frequency response of the 1.5mm device, showing a 3dB low frequency cut-off near 80 Hz.

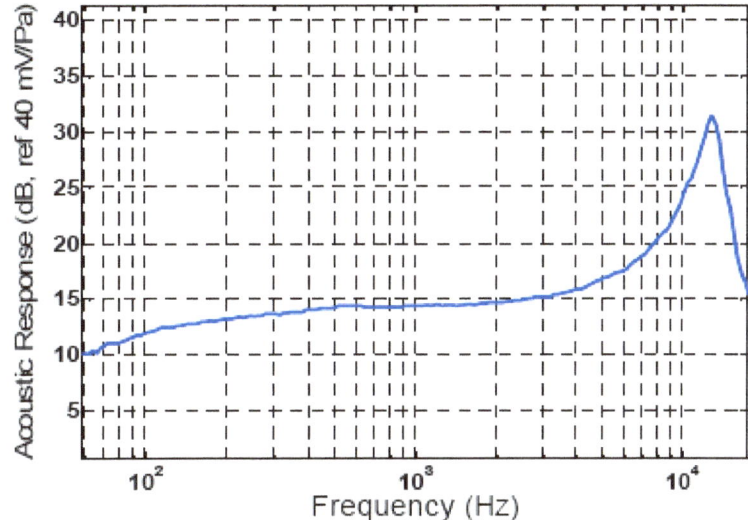

Figure 35. Acoustic response of a 2mm diameter device.

5. CONCLUSIONS

We have successfully designed, fabricated and characterized extremely high performance optical microphones during this project. These devices have volumes less than $1cm^3$, diaphragms that are 2mm or smaller and perform at the same level as reference microphones with ½ to 1 inch diameter membranes and 10 to 100 times the volume. In terms of acoustic measurements, these microphones have ~20 dBA internal noise, pressure resolution of $<1uPa/\sqrt{Hz}$ and a displacement resolution of 40 femtometer/$\sqrt{Hz}$. These devices have also inspired and influenced the design of novel accelerometer, inclinometer, gyro and magnetometer designs.

5.1 Publications

- "Surface and Bulk silicon micromachined optical displacement sensor fabricated with SwIFT-lite process", N. A. Hall, M. Okandan, F.L. Degertekin, IEEE JMEMS, v.15, n.4, pg.770, Aug. 2006

- "Impact of relative intensity noise of vertical cavity surface emitting lasers on optics based micromachined audio and seismic sensors", R. Littrell, N.A. Hall, M. Okandan, R. Olsson, D. Serkland, Applied Optics, to be published Oct. 2007

- "Finite-element based thin-film damping model and thermal mechanical noise spectra simulations for advanced micromachined microphone structures", N.A. Hall, R. Littrell, M. Okandan, B. Bicen, F. L. Degertekin, IEEE JMEMS, submitted

5.2 Presentations

- "Surface and Bulk microfabrication of optical seismometers and vibrometers using Sandia National Laboratories' silicon micromachining technology", M. Okandan, N.A. Hall, R. Littrell, B. Bicen, F.L. Degertekin, Acoustical Society of America, Annual Meeting, Honolulu, HI, Dec. 2006

- "Finite-element modeling of thin-film damping in micromachined microphones employing diffraction based optical readout", N. A. Hall, M. Okandan, F. L. Degertekin, Acoustical Society of America, Annual Meeting, Honolulu, HI, Dec. 2006

- "Optical microphone structures fabricated for broad bandwidth and low noise", M. Okandan, N.A. Hall, B. Bicen, C. Garcia, F. L. Degertekin, IEEE Sensors'07, Oct. 29 2007, Atlanta, GA

- "A low noise, fully packaged micromachined grating based optical microphone", N.A. Hall, B. Bicen, C. Garcia, M. Okandan, F.L. Degertekin, IEEE MEMS'08, submitted

5.3 Technical Advances

- 10082   Tuned Optical Cavity Sensor – Micro FTIR
- 10094   Microinterferometric Sensor Platform
- 10306   Interferometric Combined Accelerometer/Rate Sensor
- 10458   Fabrication and integration of interferometric sensor
- 10346   Lensless integration of interferometry based sensor platform

5.4 Programmatic Outlook / Complementary Projects

The fundamental sensing technique that forms the basis of the optical microphone has been utilized in several different projects, leading to novel accelerometer, gyro and magnetometer designs. Further development of these concepts are possible, through other LDRDs and possible collaboration with industrial partners and customers.

During the course of this project, we have also made contact with DoD customers (Infantry Center at Fort Benning, GA), which generated significant interest and initial system requirements for a dismounted counter-sniper system. We are also continuing to explore other possibilities with DARPA and other agencies for further development of the sensors and systems enabled by these sensors.

Distribution

1	MS0959	Ken Peterson	2452
1	MS1004	Eric Parker	6344
5	MS1080	Murat Okandan	1749
1	MS1080	Paul Resnick	1749
1	MS1085	Darwin Serkland	1742
2	MS9018	Central Technical Files	8944
2	MS0899	Technical Library	4536
1	MS0123	D. Chavez, LDRD Office	1011

www.ingramcontent.com/pod-product-compliance
Lightning Source LLC
Chambersburg PA
CBHW041524280526
45792CB00004B/1374